# Foreclosure Cleanout E

*"Everything you need to get started"*

## National Client List Included

## AUTHOR

## James R. Tolliver

ISBN-13: 978-0615551371
ISBN-10: 0615551378

*James R. Tolliver*

# Foreclosure Cleanout Business

# Starting a Trashout/Preservation Business

## First thing is first

Pick a name that is not being used and do a name availability search with the Secretary of State Office. Then incorporate to protect yourself from potential law suits.

Once you have incorporated, get a Federal and State Tax Id number. This will allow you open a bank account.

Once you have gotten your Federal Tax Id and bank account, now it is time to start applying for field asset insurance. Please review the insurance section of the contractors manual for suggested limits and companies who offer that type of insurance.

## List of must have tools

Basic Tools (Hammers, screw drivers, wrenches, etc.)

Camera

Gps

Computer/Printer

High Speed Internet for fast uploading pictures

Truck, large trailer – Be prepared for trashouts that are as small as a pick up load and trashouts as large as the biggest one we ever did, this one was 7 large dumpsters (40 yard dumpsters) almost 300 yards in total.

Generator

Extension cords

Cordless drills, saws, etc.

Air compressor

Pry bars/Hammers/Screw drivers/Drill bits/Pump to pump out pools
Rakes/Shovels

Riding Mower (Commercial Mower is better)

Weed eater

Chain Saw

Hedge trimmer

Wheel barrel

Step Ladder

26 ft extension ladder

Cleaning supplies, buckets, mops, etc.

Water containers to carry about 20 gallons in total

Flashlights and lanterns

Now that you have a name, a Federal Tax Id number, insurance, and tools, it is time to market for preservation work.

## Marketing

## The absolute best way to get business is to sign up as a vendor with national Reo Asset Management Companies.

Target local agents who specialize in foreclosures. These can be found on foreclosed homes for sale. **Note, drive around in neighborhoods to find those agents**

Target nationwide reo asset management companies, property preservation and management companies. I have a list included in this packet with (Names and contact information for the larger nationwide clients)

Lastly build a web site and get listed in the phone book.

## Once you get accepted

Let me save you money and time. I have enclosed a list of places to get
supplies that you will need in order to do your job. There are specific key
codes for locks, door knobs, and dead bolts. DO NOT GO TO A HARDWARE STORE AND STOCK UP. You must order

these from companies that specifically make the knobs and locks for this industry.

Now you need an accounting system. If you do it manual, list the dates, work order number, property address, and the amount of the invoice. These companies and banks are not responsible for keeping up with what they owe you.

I used QuickBooks and this was very efficient, even though most of these companies have their own billing system.  This way you can track what and how much you were paid.

## Performing initial Services

The things included in the initial services are usually as follows;

Trashout (Interior and Exterior debris removal)

Maid Service (Sales Clean)

Boarding up broken windows

Winterization (Winterization Season is Oct 1$^{st}$ through March 31$^{st}$)

Tarp the roof if leaking

Initial Grass Cut (Includes trimming and edging)

Capping exposed wires (Depends on client)

Capping gas lines (Depends on client)

Installation of handrails (Depends on client)

Bidding items that are safety issues or requested by client.

This is the end of the introduction. You will find many things included in this guide to be most helpful.

Contractors Manual on what's expected as far as Insurance, "How To's", picture taking, etc.

Industry Standard Pricing (To be used as a guide when bidding jobs)

Maid Service/Sales Clean Checklist

Winterization Check List

Boarding a window example

Supplier list

## **Best of All;**

***List of Clients that you will need to get set up with that can jump start your business. ***

*Good Luck and don't be afraid to get dirty*

# Contractors Manual

This is general guide of the function and how to perform the role of a Preservation/Trashout Contractor .

The following are technological tools that is required for contractors
Cell Phone
E-mail Capabilities
Digital camera
Answering machine
Fax machine
Scanner
Wireless Service

## A Brief Overview

Clients include mortgage lenders and mortgage servicing companies throughout the United States. Most contractors performs a variety of services to its clients. Contractors can performs property inspections, property preservation, appraisals and title/document retrieval, hazard claim insurance recovery, itemized estimates of damages and complete property repairs. The following is a short overview of each department's functions.

## Property Inspections

Monthly Property Inspections
Collection Interviews
Pre-Foreclosure Notification
Sale Date Inspections
24 Hour Rush Inspections
Loss Mitigation Verification Inspections
Commercial Property Inspections
Occupancy checks Special projects

## Property Preservation
Contractor  may provide one, several or all services to a client., including:
Initial securing
Winterization

Monthly grass cuts
Clear for conveyance/sale
Eviction/move-out assistance
Environmental studies
REO trash-outs

## Appraisal/BPO/Title Document Retrieval

Drive-by Appraisals
Full interior appraisals
Broker's Opinion - Freddie Mac and Fannie Mae approved Title
search/Limited title search
Assignment Filing

## Hazard Insurance Claim Recovery / Repairs

Claims: filing, negotiation, settlement Adjuster's Scope Verification
Coverage Opinions
Repair Estimates
Repair/Project Management

## Types and Amounts of Insurance Required

Comprehensive General Liability, Errors and Omissions,
Non-Owned & Hired Auto Liability coverage as well as Workers
Compensation coverage. In order for Contractors to begin and continue
business with many clients, Contractors and their subcontractors are required
to carry, at all times and at their own expense, the following minimum

INSURANCE COVERAGE:

1) Commercial General Liability in the amount of $1 million per
occurrence/$1 million
Aggregate including:
• Personal injury/Advertising injury protection
• Care/Custody/Control coverage in the amount of $50,000
• Products/Completed Operations
2) Errors & Omissions' in the amount of $1 million per occurrence/$1
million aggregate
Covering:
• Residential property inspections
• Delinquent borrower interviews
• Commercial property inspections
• Insurance loss inspections

- Eviction services
- Property preservation inspections
- Property preservation estimates
- Property preservation services (including but not limited to REO services)
- Property repair estimates
- Property rehabilitation services
- Merchant site verifications

**Note**: Please make sure that the Errors & Omissions insurance coverage is not from a Professional Liability policy that a realtor or lawyer would carry, as there are significant differences between the two policies regarding covered risks and expectations. Some companies that offer this coverage for field services are listed below:

York Jersey Underwriters (800-392-6958)
Leonard Insurance (800-451-1904)

3) Automobile Liability, including bodily injury liability, property damage liability, and uninsured motorist coverage, for all owned, non-owned and hired vehicles, in the amount of $1 million combined single limit.

4) Employer's Liability Insurance with limits of $1 million per occurrence.

5) Workers' Compensation as provided by statute.

## E & O Insurance

All Subcontractors are required to purchase Contractor/Inspector Liability Insurance
Inspectors to carry total limits of no
less than $1,000,000 Errors and Omissions coverage.

## Reasons To Carry This Insurance

The examples below illustrate the need for Errors and Omissions Insurance coverage for Subcontractors:

Someone is injured: You fail to report a hazardous condition (i.e. broken steps) at the property and, as a result, someone hurts themselves.

Damages occur: You reported a property as occupied when it was actually vacant and damages occur (i.e. tree fell through roof, mold is growing or flooding occurs).

A violation is posted: You fail to report a violation posted for debris/grass which may cause you to be responsible for the cost to abate the violation.

Homeowner's Insurance cancellation: You report the property as vacant when it was actually occupied. The Homeowner's Insurance may be cancelled because of this. You may be responsible for the loss not covered due to the mortgagor not having insurance (flooding, fire or theft) or for the cost to reinstate the insurance.

A subcontractor performs the work: Although you subcontract work it is important to keep in mind that you are still responsible for all guidelines provided in this manual.

## General Guidelines:

Photos must support all work performed and/or the bid submitted.

If you are billing a charge and have no photos to support that charge, you may not be paid.

Before/During and After photos are required of each item of work performed.

Please arrange the photos in a logical work order sequence when placing them on the web for most clients. For example, before showing window broken and after showing window replaced.

Photos must be submitted in color not in black and white. If a photo submitted is unclear, too light/dark or is not sufficient, and cannot be resent via the web, another photo must be taken and the contractor may not be paid for the return trip.

Since contractors use digital cameras to update photos directly to the website, please purge your camera of previous photos before transmitting to the client. Make sure that you are renaming the new photos with the correct work order number.

## What does REO mean?

An REO (Real Estate Owned) property is one that has gone through foreclosure and that the bank has bought at the foreclosure sale. The bank now officially owns the property, and it is being marketed for sale.

## Clients' Objective:

These properties will have to be marketed and sold by the client for them to recoup their initial investment in the property. Every day that our clients cannot market or sell their properties is costing them money.

## Clients' Goals:

Every client's REO Department has set a goal to place a property on the market within days of acquisition.

## What is the Contractor's Role?

As an REO contractor, you are the eyes and ears of the client in the field. Contractors are more often than not the first individuals to see the true condition of a property. Being the clients "eyes and ears" means contractors must photograph and document damages, hazards and dangerous conditions, which you may encounter at the properties. Therefore, if the property has fire damages and the floors are not safe to walk on, the client needs to know about it prior to the Agent showing the property to a potential buyer.

## What is marketable condition?

Placing a property into marketable condition requires the following:
   Timely securing
   Complete exterior and interior debris removal (referred to as the trashout)

Winterization (when/where applicable)
Maid Services (often referred to as a sales clean)
Lawn Maintenance

## Personal/Financial Papers:
## Examples
## IMPORTANT: These types of papers and documents must be treated as personal property, regardless of quantity or condition.

They include, but are not limited to:
Records, and certificates of any kind, including but not limited to:
  Birth
  Death
  Tax
  Military
  School including report cards, diplomas, school books, software, disks (hard or floppy)
  Health and insurance paperwork
  Business records
  Deeds, Liens, other legal papers
  Files and file folders
  Lockboxes and safes
  Mail of any kind
When in doubt, treat the item as a personal.

## Where are these personals found?
File cabinets: In some instances, personal papers are housed in file cabinets. In that case, open all drawers **and** photograph the contents of each drawer. No matter what is in the cabinets, do not touch or remove the items at this time. Report the cabinet and the contents as personals.

Boxes: Sometimes personal papers are housed in boxes, with or without lids. Follow the above instructions for file cabinets.

Bags or other containers. Sometimes personal papers of the kinds described above may be found in vinyl bags, paper bags or other similar containers. Follow the above instructions for file cabinets Loose/No container of any type. Personal papers may be loose and/or strewn about. Photograph them as found, do not touch or disturb the papers, and report as personals.

## Storage requirements

These will depend on the client. You should call the client for further instructions.

## Trashouts    (Protect yourself- Photos, Photos, and more Photos)

• Take BEFORE photos of debris at the property show entire room with debris, not just small areas of the room.

• Take photos of debris AFTER removal to show debris has been cleared. Photos should be of same area and angle as BEFORE photos.

• Final photo should be of contractor's full truckload or full dumpster load.

• For personal property: must also include approximate value and bid to remove, store and dispose.

• If you are only removing health hazards, if possible, show the health hazards in a pile, and then removed.

• If the debris can cause a citation or you are trying to show personal property, (to support your recommending an eviction of personals) take photos to support.

Photos of trashouts must include before photos of debris at the property, and after photos of the same locations once the debris has been removed. Photos of debris loaded into the trailer are not acceptable as the only after photos.

Ensuring that a property is in marketable condition and appealing to buyers is of the utmost importance. Maid service must be done in a very thorough manner and inspected by the contractor upon completion. Below is a listing of the tasks involved in a thorough maid service cleaning.

Clean all baseboards, doors, light-switch and outlet covers, light fixtures (including ceiling fans/blades), and heat and air vents/ducts. Remove any dirty non-washable window covers.

Clear cobwebs from ceilings, walls, light fixtures, fans, windows, doors, entryways, porches, and walkways.

Clean all kitchen and bathroom counter tops, cabinets, and drawers to remove dirt, smudges, grime, and debris. Leave drawers and cabinets open until final inspection.

Clean sinks and appliances (inside and out) throughout premises.

Clean kitchens and bathrooms thoroughly, including all fixtures and surfaces (toilets, tubs, showers, mirrors, etc.), using a disinfectant cleaner (one that does NOT leave a residue) to remove dirt, grime, mildew, and odor.

Clean toilets, toilet bowls, and surrounding areas thoroughly. Tape down toilet seat lids on winterized properties when finished.

Clean full-view glass doors at front and rear entries. Clean interior side of glass in windows to remove dirt, grime, fingerprints, tape, stickers, etc. Clean window ledges to remove dirt, smudges, cobwebs, dead insects, and grime.

Broom sweep interior floors, wet mop vinyl floors, and vacuum carpeted floors and rugs to present neat appearance. Be sure to include stairs, closets, baseboards, and other similar areas.

Place one (1) air freshener in every kitchen and one (1) in each bathroom.

Pine, lemon, or floral scents are acceptable.

Broom sweep porches, garages or carports, and entries leading into property to present a neat appearance.

Sweep out fireplaces and/or fireboxes to remove ashes or residue. Close damper.

Pick up and properly dispose of ALL debris from interior

The checklist located on the following pages must be filled out by each crew performing initial services on REO properties and sent to the client.

## Fannie Mae   REO Maid Services Checklist

All items must be initialed (or write N/A if a particular item is not applicable) and the form must be signed at the bottom. This is a required part of your work order, and it must be submitted via the vendor web before we can close the order. Please also see the list of required maid service photos (separate text), which must be submitted before we can close the work order. *All properties must pass the "white glove test."* As a reminder, you must call the listing agent and advise when the trashout and maid services have been completed. It is imperative that you do so, as the agents then need to inspect the property and fill out the broker sign off sheet.

The following photos are required to document the completion of maid services. Please use this as a checklist for your own reference.

example, if you note that there is no stove, we will not ask for a photo.

___ "Before/During/After" kitchen sink clean
___ "Before/During/After" kitchen counters clean
___ "Before/During/After" kitchen cabinets and drawers clean (show them with doors/drawers open)
___ "Before/During/After" kitchen floor clean
___ "Before/During/After" exterior refrigerator clean
___ "Before/During/After" interior refrigerator clean
___ "Before/During/After" exterior stove clean
___ "Before/During/After" interior oven clean

___ "Before/After" dishwasher (door open, showing that it is empty and clean)
___ "Before/During/After" bathroom sinks and fixtures clean

___ "Before/During/After" toilets and toilet bowls clean (if winterizing, use photos of antifreeze in toilet bowls as the "after" maid service photos, as toilets must be cleaned before antifreeze is added)

___ "Before/During/After" bath tubs and shower areas clean

___ "Before/During/After" bathroom floors clean

___ "Before/During/After" closets cleaned out and vacuumed/mopped

___ "Before/During/After" ceiling fans clean/free of dust

___ "Before/During/After" baseboards, windows, window sills, corners of walls, cobwebs removed

___ "Before/During/After" fireplace clean

___ "Before/During/After" all floors swept/mopped or vacuumed

___ "Before/During/After" cleaning air vents, ducts

___ "Before/During/After" cleaning porches, patios, garages, carports


In order to ensure the comprehensiveness of our service delivery to our REO clients, i.e. Hud requires monthly maid refreshes on all Cradle to Grave properties. New refresh orders are opened every 30 days after the completion of initial services. In order to efficiently and effectively complete the maid refresh services, all contractors will be required to maintain a maid refresh list (similar to that of the grass cut list) and utilize a separate maid service crew to perform the service.


Work order instructions include the following:
- Wipe down counters and cupboards
- Clean windows and window sills
- Clean all sinks, tubs and toilets
- Vacuum carpets
- Mop floors

Call from site to obtain approval for any of the following that may be needed and be prepared to do the work:
- Securing
- Debris Removal
- Shrubs
- Grass
- Emergency repairs

The following MAID SERVICE 'REFRESH' photos are required:

Each refresh require a minimum of 35 photos: as many during photos as needed per work completed, with before and after photos as well (multi-unit properties will require more)

Mandatory photos on each order will be the water meter, all toilets (with lids up) and main water value zip tied in the off position to ensure the winterization is in tact    All horizontal surfaces must be wiped down with cleaning chemicals (including, but not limited to, counters, fan blades, window sills, etc) Also including floors; carpets must be vacuumed and hard surfaces must be mopped (as needed). Please also include a photo of all sinks and tubs to ensure they are in a clean condition.

If a room is clean and does not need a refresh, a general condition photo of the entire room from opposite angles is needed to ensure proof that further cleaning is not needed.

Photos cannot all be up-close, need condition photos of entire room

In order to ensure that properties show well, it is imperative that light bulbs are replaced in common areas. Please follow the instructions below when addressing light bulbs in REO properties:
If electricity is off:

♉   Replace any missing light bulbs in common areas listed below:

## Interior Areas Exterior Areas
Basement Entryway(s) to house
Bathrooms Front porch
Bedrooms Security lights
Dining rooms
Family/Living rooms
Hallways
Kitchens
Stairways
If electricity is on:
♉   Replace any burnt out light bulbs in common areas listed below:

## Interior Areas Exterior Areas

Basement Entryway(s) to house
Bathrooms Front porch
Bedrooms Security lights
Dining rooms
Family/Living rooms
Hallways
Kitchens
Stairways

Cut lawn to property edge and to a maximum height of 3 inches, or to requirements of local code, or consistent with adjacent/surrounding properties, unless otherwise instructed by clients. All grass clippings must be removed from the lawn, sidewalks, steps, etc.

Trim shrubs away from house, walkways, and entrances. Sweep or otherwise clear all paved surfaces. Edge all paved surfaces and trim around all trees, bushes, fences, foundations, and planting beds.

(1) BEFORE and (1) AFTER of front yard and (1) BEFORE and AFTER of rear yard from same angle.
-Photos of BEFORE and AFTER should show the same area and be from the same angle. All AFTER photos should show the clippings raked up and removed.
Photos of fence line trimmed.
Photos to support that clippings were removed from yard, driveway, sidewalks and walkways.
Photo to show property was edged.
To support an oversize lot charge, more photos may be required- but try to minimize the number of photos by stepping back to get more of the lot in the photo. If grass does not need cutting due to limited growth, we still require photos showing the limited growth but we will only need 2 photos maximum, 1 of the front of the yard and 1 of the rear yard.

If the grass cannot be cut because the property is occupied or is being maintained by another

party, the client still need photos of the front of the house showing the address.

The client will not be able to pay you for a grass cut performed if any of the photos show that the ground is covered in snow.

If you are bidding the grass cut, your photos must support the bid.

If a for sale sign needs to be moved to cut the grass, it must be replaced after the cut is completed.

Snow removal is ordered by Brokers on an as needed basis and must be completed within 48 hours

Snow removal is to be completed per the city ordinances - walkways, sidewalks and entryways are to be cleared.

Please read work orders to follow specific guidelines that the client may have a cash for keys order is when the client is willing to pay the occupant to vacate the property, to avoid an eviction. The client now owns this property. In order to perform a cash for keys order, it is necessary to visit the property in the evening when it is more likely that someone will be home. A dollar range that can be negotiated will be provided on the order. Please advise the occupant that the client now owns the property, and they are interested in making an offer to the occupant to vacate the property in exchange for a check. Please also explain to the occupants that as part of this agreement, they will be expected to clear out the property and clean it, so that it is in marketable condition. This means that all debris and personals must be removed, and the interior must be wiped down. Failure to do so will result in the client not giving them the check.

Call the REO department immediately and advise on the success of your efforts. If the mortgagor counter offers, please let them know that amount. The client needs to be informed for the entire process.

You may need to make multiple trips to establish contact, so please let them know each time you go out and when you can make another trip. They will also provide a notice that you can leave at the property if you are not able to make direct contact. Place this in an envelope and tape it to the door.

Cash for keys offers can be extended to tenants and mortgagors alike. Once the occupants agree to an amount, you must set a date and time to return with their check.

Preferably the appointment will be set within two weeks of their agreeing to the deal. You may give them up to three weeks if necessary, but anything beyond three weeks requires the client's approval. You must notify the client immediately if the occupants require more than three weeks to move.

A cash for keys order and the property is vacant, please call the client immediately.

Contractors will be paid for successful cash for keys orders only.
If you believe that the property is already vacant, call the client and advise.

Do not remove anything from the property at that time.

All bids must be justified with photo documentation and complete descriptions of the work that must be performed.
New photos must always be provided on work per bid completions

Property condition reports must be filled out the client for all work orders within 24 hours of completion.

It is imperative that all updates contain complete information regarding all completed work

Clients requires 2 completed dates on Reo Initial Service orders , the date the property was secured and the date the trashout was completed.

Updates must always address damages. If there is no reference to damages on the update, the work order will remain open until that information is obtained. If damages are found, include a description and cause of damages as well as an eyeball estimate to repair.

Eyeball estimates are not bids to repair

Calling the client from site once the property is secured is required. In addition, a call must be made to the broker as well as an email sent to advise the property is secured and then repeated after the trashout has been completed.

## Broker Sign Off Sheet

Please assist the client in better serving your properties. Below is a checklist of the work we have recently completed on your listing. We would appreciate it if you could provide feedback, to ensure the best possible quality. Please circle the appropriate rating below each category, and include any comments at the bottom of the form.
Work Completed:
- Clear interior, including cleaning: Includes all trash and health hazards, as well as the interior cleaning. Property should be in "broom swept" condition, with all surfaces wiped clean, windows wiped down, fan blades cleaned, floors mopped (and vacuumed if electricity is on), and so on. This service does not include professionally cleaning or shampooing carpets, replacing any fixtures or outlet covers, fixing any damages on the interior, or replacing light bulbs

EXCELLENT GOOD FAIR POOR NOT DONE/NOT APPLICABLE
- Clear exterior of debris: Includes all debris and hazards present; all items should have been removed from the property entirely.
EXCELLENT GOOD FAIR POOR NOT DONE/NOT APPLICABLE
- Lock changes/lock box: All locks are to be changed, including knobs and deadbolts, and padlocks should be used to secure sheds, garages, and outbuildings. A lock box should be present, and working keys to open all locks must be inside the lock box.
EXCELLENT GOOD FAIR POOR NOT DONE/NOT APPLICABLE
- Grass cut: Includes edging along walkways and driveway, using a weed eater on weeds along the foundation. On larger lots, a perimeter cut of 100'x100' may be completed. This also includes shrub trimming, as needed.
EXCELLENT GOOD FAIR POOR NOT DONE/NOT APPLICABLE

- Additional securing, if needed: May include boarding of windows or door openings.
EXCELLENT GOOD FAIR POOR NOT DONE/NOT APPLICABLE
- Winterization, if applicable: Includes a system shutdown, draining the hot water tank, blowing excess water out of the lines, adding antifreeze to all traps, and posting winterization tags throughout the property.
EXCELLENT GOOD FAIR POOR NOT DONE/NOT APPLICABLE
Comments:

_____

_____

_____

_____

_____

I, _____, the local broker,

_____ Agree the above work has been satisfactorily completed.

_____ Disagree the above work has been satisfactorily completed

Signature: _____

Date: _____


Photos are required of all posted stickers. Stickers are to be placed on glass surfaces. Care should be taken as to not cover any vacancy stickers.

# SECURING NOTICE
## UTILITY WINTERIZATION NOTICE
Please note that this property has been winterized. No utilities should be turned on without a walk-through inspection of the property to ensure that all faucets and valves are in the off position. Prior to turning on the electricity, you need to ensure the breaker for the hot water tank is in the "off" position. Failure to complete a thorough walk through of the home may result in damage to the property. Be sure to check on the following:
- Utilities on and functioning properly?
- Sump pump plugged in and operable?
- Breakers off (except breaker for sump pump, if applicable)?

- Faucets/spigots off, including exterior spigots?

- Stove and oven turned off?
- Lights turned off?
- Any other issues that require attention, including damages?
If you have any questions, please call

_____

At this number the number below:

_____

Thank you.
## WINTERIZATION NOTICE

# REO ASSET MANAGEMNET COMPANIES

**The absolute best way to build your business. Note, they are difficult to please, but they are worth working with due to the volume of business that they have to offer.**

These are the top companies that covers the entire nation.

**S A F E G U A R D   P R O P E R T I E S ,   L L C**
Property Preservation Department
7887 SAFEGUARD CIRCLE
VALLEY VIEW OH 44125
Phone: 1-800-852-8306

**Keystone Asset Management, Inc.**
3015 Advance Ln, Colmar, PA 18915
Phone: 215.855.3350 Fax: 267.308.2118

**Cyprexx**
1 (800) 516-6348
vendorsupport@cyprexx.com

**Field Assets**
Toll Free 800-468-1743
Local 512-467-1537
Fax 512-467-1639 24/7

**New Vista Asset Management**
15010 Avenue of Science, Suite 200
San Diego, CA 92128
Tel. (858) 432-5200
Fax. (858) 432-5252
Toll Free. (877) 342-7028
info@nvam.net

# Other Reo Asset Management Companies

The area that you live will depend on which of these companies may operate. Don't be afraid to search the internet for new companies starting to do business in your area.

Many of the companies listed below are searchable by the internet to see if they actual do business in your area. Don't waste your time filling out the long application if they don't service your area.

- **FAS Financial Asset Services Inc.**
- **Excellent REO**
- **National Default Servicing**
- **Olympus Asset Management Inc**
- **REO Experts**
- **Integrated Asset Services**
- **REO World**
- **Equity Pointe**
- **LAMCO**
- **Bankers Asset Management**
- **NREIS Asset Management**
- **New Vista Asset Management**
- **Corporate Asset Management, LLC**
- **Platinum Real Estate Services, Inc.**
- **J.E.M. REO Resources, Inc.**
- **National REO Services, Inc.**
- **REO Solutions**
- **Precision Asset Management**
- **Archon Group**
- **REO Nationwide**
- **HUD**
- **Bank of America**
- **Premiere Asset Services (Wells Fargo)**

**Maid Services Checklist**

- **Entry Way:**

- ___ Floor swept/mopped

- ___ Cobwebs removed from corners/ceiling

- ___ Baseboards, walls wiped down

- ___ Light fixtures, switch and outlet covers wiped down

- ___ Storm door glass cleaned


- **Living Room:**

- ___ Floor swept/mopped or carpet vacuumed

- ___ Cobwebs removed from corners/ceiling

- ___ Baseboards, walls wiped down

- ___ Light fixtures, switch and outlet covers wiped down

- ___ Windows clean, window sills wiped off

- ___ Door frames free of dust

- ___ Fireplace cleaned out (if applicable)

- ___ Ceiling fan blades clean


- **Family Room:**

- ___ Floor swept/mopped or carpet vacuumed

- ___ Cobwebs removed from corners/ceiling
- ___ Light fixtures, switch and outlet covers wiped down
- ___ Windows clean, window sills wiped off
- ___ Door frames free of dust
- ___ Fireplace cleaned out (if applicable)
- ___ Ceiling fan blades clean


- **Kitchen:**
- ___ Sink cleaned
- ___ Stove/oven cleaned (inside and out)
- ___ Microwave cleaned (inside and out)
- ___ Dishwasher cleaned (inside and out)
- ___ Refrigerator cleaned (inside and out)
- ___ Floor swept and mopped
- ___ Windows cleaned, window sills wiped off
- ___ Counters clean
- ___ Cobwebs removed from corners/ceiling
- ___ Baseboards, walls wiped down
- ___ Light fixtures, switch and outlet covers wiped down
- ___ Ceiling fan blades clean
- **Bedrooms** (Number of bedrooms: ____)

- ___ Floor swept/mopped or carpet vacuumed

- ___ Cobwebs removed from corners/ceiling

- ___ Baseboards, walls wiped down

- ___ Light fixtures, switch and outlet covers wiped down

- ___ Windows clean, window sills wiped off

- ___ Door frames free of dust

- ___ Ceiling fan blades clean

- ___ Closet floors swept/mopped or vacuumed

- **Bathrooms** (Number of bathrooms: ___ full and ___ half):

- ___ Floor swept/mopped

- ___ Cobwebs removed from corners/ceiling

- ___ Baseboards, walls wiped down

- ___ Toilets clean

- ___ Tub/shower and surrounding area clean, free of any dust

- ___ Mirrors, cabinets, drawers, shelves clean

**Porches/Deck Areas/All Paved Surfaces:**

- ___ Swept free of debris

- ___ All leaves, sticks, and any other debris removed

- **Garage:**

- ___ Swept free of debris

- ___ All leaves, sticks, and any other debris removed

- ___ Free of all debris, swept out

- ___ Cobwebs removed from corners/ceiling


- **Additional Services Required:**

- ___ Installed air freshener – kitchen, bathroom and laundry room

- *mark with installation date

- ___ Installed batteries in smoke detectors when needed

- ___ Installed light bulbs in all open sockets and replaced

non functioning light bulbs


- **Notes:**

# Winterization Check List

Contractor Code:_____     Utilities (Meter Reading)
Property Address:_____     Water: on/off (_____)
Date:_____     Electric:on/off (_____)
Employee's Name_____     Gas: on/off (_____)

List Any Additional Information:
_____
_____
_____

***Document any pre-existing plumbing system and/or water damages to the property:

***Attention Contractors*** It is important for each contractor to provide photo documentation which
supports each step during the winterization process. Please remember to provide and illustrate in-depth
photos which highlight each step on the Winterization checklist.

**Disconnecting Water Supply Pressure Test System**
___Shut water off at the curb
system.
___Install Zip tie on main shut off valve
___Was water meter disconnected?
___Was Main water line pluged?
___Photo documentation of all the above?
___Photo documentation of all the above?

**Draining the System**
___Shut off gas or electric to Water Heater
___Drain Water Heater (outside or floor drain) and tanks)
___Drain Well/Holding tanks if applicable
___Disconnect electric to well pump if applicable
___Drain all toilet tanks and bowls above?
___Photo documentation of all the above?

**Blowing the lines**
___Close all faucets and valves
___Attach compressor (5 gallon or 3.8 CF )
___Build pressure to 35 PSI
___Open 1 faucet valve at a time (hot then cold).
___Did air/water come out of every faucet/valve?
___Is all water out of the system?
___Photo documentation of all the above?
___NO wint sticker on door.
***Provide a detailed reason why the system doesn't hold pressure_____
above?

___Make sure all water is drained from

___Close all faucet/valves.
___Build pressure to 35 PSI
___Did pressure hold for 30 mins?
___Document why it didn't hold pressure.

**Adding Anti-Freeze**
___Add anti-freeze to all toilets (bowls

___Add anti-freeze to all sinks
___Add anti-freeze to all Shower/Tub
___Photo documentation of all the
___Add anti-freeze to dish washer

**Stickers**
___Wint sticker on toilets.
___Wint sticker on Tubs/Showers
___Wint sticker on water heater.
___Wint sticker on water meter.
___Wint sticker on dish washer.
___Wint sticker on sinks.

___Toilet wrap installed on toilets.
___Photo documentation of all the

# Boarding Example

## PLYWOOD BOARDING PANEL DETAIL

### NO SCALE

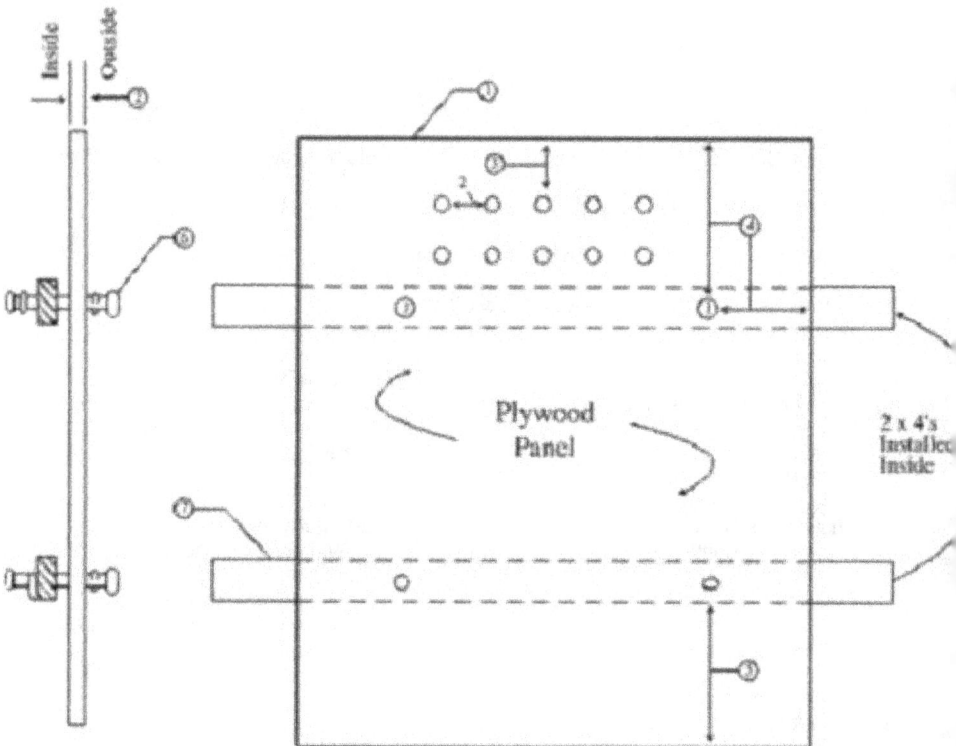

Inside | Outside

Plywood
Panel

2 x 4's
Installed
Inside

BEFORE and AFTER photos of each window or door unless you are boarding the entire property. In that case, step back and take a BEFORE photo of the whole front of the house, and then an AFTER photo showing the front of the house boarded. Then do that same on the back and sides of the house. The client does not need a close up before and after photos of every window on complete board ups from the exterior. It is required to show before and after photos of every window from the interior.

# Invoice

Contractor Name  _____          Date  [        ]

Address  _____

Phone  _____

Email  _____

Client

|  |
|  |

Property Address

|  |
|  |

Work Description                                      Price

|  |  |
|  |  |

Total  [        ]

# Work Order

Contractor Name _____        Date [        ]

Address _____

Phone _____

Email _____

Client

Property Address

Work Description

# Photo Requirements (General Clients)
# Not to be confused with Fannie Mae

| **Trashout**<br>**Photos #**<br>**needed** | **Photos Before** |
|---|---|
| All | All interior and exterior trash<br>The more the better<br>Have to justify billing |
| All | All interior and exterior trash<br>The more the better<br>Have to justify billing |
| | **During** |
| 6-10 | Carrying debris out at least 6 |
| | **After** |
| 10 | After Debits is cleared from inside and out |

| **Maid Service**<br>**Photos #**<br>**needed** | **Job** |
|---|---|
| | **Before Photos** |
| 10 | All Rooms |
| | **During Photos** |
| 2 | Sweeping floors |
| 1 | Mopping floors |
| 1 | Clearing Counter Top |
| 2 | Dusting Corners |
| 1 | Cleaning Window sills |

**After**

| | |
|---|---|
| 1 | Kitchen sink |
| 1 | Bath Sink |
| 1 | Bath Tub |
| 1 | Ceiling Fans |
| 1 | Window sill |
| 2 | Inside kitchen cabinets |
| 1 | Dishwasher |
| 1 | Stove |
| 1 | Toilet with lid up |
| 1 | Dirty Mop water |
| 1 | Water meter or hot water valve zip tied |
| 1 | Air Freshener with the date |

## Grass Cutting

| | |
|---|---|
| 4 | Before all 4 sides |
| 4 | During all 4 sides |
| 4 | After all 4 sides |
| 2 | Drive way edge |
| 2 | Weed eating |
| 2 | Spraying Weeds |

**Other work**

Before all items are removed
After all items removed
During photos as possible
After work complete

HUD Properties.

Notice Sheet
Sign in sheet
House number
All regular pics

# Winterization

| Photos # needed | Job |
|---|---|
| 1 | Hot water heater drained |
| 1 | Water meter off/on |
| 1 | Water meter being turn off |
| 3 | Water meter after turned off |
| 3 | Water meter before zip tied |
| 1 | Toilets before cleaned |
| 1 | Toilets after cleaned |
| 1 | Sink pouring antifreeze |
| 1 | Tub pouring antifreeze |
| 1 | Dishwasher pouring antifreeze |
| 1 | Toilet pouring antifreeze |
| 1 | Toilet tank pouring antifreeze |
| 1 | Washer drain pouring antifreeze |
| 1 | Sub Pump pouring antifreeze |
| 1 | Under sinks photo showing pipes |
| 1 | Breaker box on/off before |
| 1 | Breaker box off after |
| 6 | Air compressor hooked up |
| 1 | Furnace |
| 2 | Front of house |
| 1 | Rear of House |
| 1 | Left side of house |
| 1 | Right side of house |
| 1 | Lock box on door |
| 1 | Front grass |
| 1 | Rear Grass |
| 1 | All damages |
| 1 | Safety Hazard Check List |

# Winterized

**Notice**

**This Property**

**has been winterized.**

**Water has been turned off.**

**Please do not use the toilets.**

**Date Winterized**

_____

**Contractor Information**

# Pricing Model

Lock Changes $60.00

Additional Lock Changes $35.00

Lockbox $20.00

Slide bolts/Slider Lock $20.00

Boarding 1/2 inch $0.60 /UI

Boarding 5/8 inch (Fast Track) $0.75 / UI

AZ Boarding requirements $0.80 / UI

Install Security Door $150.00

Reglazing $0.75 / UI

Dry Winterization/dewinterization $100.00

Dry Wint/dewint - add'l unit $45.00

Dry wint with sprinkler system $125.00

Steam/Radiant Winterization/dewinterization $135.00

Steam/Radiant wint/dewint- add'l unit $70.00

Steam/Radiant wint with sprinkler system $160.00

Clean and rewinterize toilet $25.00

Pressure test only $50.00

Initial Maid Service $150.00

Maid Service $75/additional unit

Monthly Marketability Order $38/unit

Auto Removal $120.00

Install Smoke Detector (each) $20.00 ea. Gross

Install CO Detector (each) $40.00 ea. Gross

Hard Wired Unit (each) $35.00

Water Heater straps $75 for 2 straps

Third party give access/wait time $25/hr; $75 max.

Install a No Trespassing Sign $5.00/per sign

Cap Initial Water Line $20.00

Cap Additional Water Line $15.00

Trashout (by the Cubic Yard) $32.50/cyd

Appliance Removal $32.50/cyd

Non-Hazardous Paint $32.50/cyd

Hazardous Paint $5 Gallon

Oil $10/gallon after 5 gallons

Household Cleaning Products $32.50/cyd

## Grass Cuts

**Length of Area Depth up to 12"**
0 - 75' $35.00
76 - 150' $50.00
151 - 200' $75.00
201 - 250' $100.00
251 - 300' $125.00

Increase price from here to suit your needs

# Pools

Pool Shock treatment $75 per visit

Larvacide Treatment (mosquito dunks) $30 per visit

Above-Ground: Drain $250.00

Above Ground: Dismantle/Remove $300.00

In-Ground: Empty Completely [to clean] $350.00

In-Ground: Clean $200.00

In-Ground: Refill Using House Utilities $200.00

In-Ground: Refill With Water Delivery Per Receipt + 10%

In-Ground: Drain to 3-4 ft. Only $200.00

In-Ground: Safety Pool Cover Pool Cover Cost [Flat] + $200.00 Fee [Discounted]

In-Ground: Winterize $350.00

# Preservation Suppliers

## <u>Locks and Specialty Supplies</u>

MFS Supply

mfssupply.com

800-607-0541


BarginLocks.com

www.bargainlocks.com

888-299-7159


## <u>General Supplies</u>

Local hardware stores –Lumber etc.

Auto Zone- Antifreeze for winterization

www.ingramcontent.com/pod-product-compliance
Lightning Source LLC
Chambersburg PA
CBHW071126210326
41519CB00020B/6435